Dim Sum BASICS

Dim Sum
BASICS

Irresistible Bite-sized Snacks Made Easy

Ng Lip Kah

mc **Marshall Cavendish**
Cuisine

CONTENTS

SMALL DISHES

RICE and SAVOURY CAKES

PASTRIES and DESSERTS

INTRODUCTION

Dim sum is a Cantonese phrase that refers to an assortment of food, each prepared in portions smaller than a main meal. In Mandarin, dim sum is called *dian xin*, which literally translates to "touch the heart". The origin of this name has never been explicitly documented or explained.

There are various kinds of Chinese cuisine, and dim sum is one of them. While the food in different parts of China do include dim sum snacks, the concept of serving dim sum is the most developed in Cantonese cuisine. Traditional dim sum includes steamed buns, dumplings and rice rolls. Today, the variety has expanded to include roast pork, various types of porridge and soups, and most dim sum eateries will serve these items. Dim sum snacks are usually served in threes or fours, with the steamed snacks like *siew mai* and *har kow* in classic steamer baskets, and the sweet baked pastries on plates.

Enjoying dim sum is part of Chinese culture, and includes the standard practice of having steamed buns, shrimp dumplings, pork dumplings, rice rolls and so on. Most of the time, they are served hot, with only a handful of cold dishes. For example, the dessert, snow skin dumplings on page 87, are best served chilled.

Northern China is looked upon as the main producer of dough products, and they are credited with the creation of numerous pastries. While this has an important influence on dim sum, the southern Chinese has also contributed to the dim sum variety. Southern Chinese dim sum can be broadly categorised into savoury and sweet snacks, most of which are covered in this book.

As with all kinds of Chinese cuisine, different cooking techniques are employed to prepared dim sum. Sometimes, two or more cooking techniques are used for one dish. Some of the key techniques used in this book are briefly explained in the following pages.

Dim sum snacks come in different shapes and sizes. Depending on the region from which it originated, the same food item may have a different shape. For example, soup dumplings (*xiao long bao*) from the southern regions of China are dented at the top, unlike the ones in the north, which peak nicely at the top where all the pleats meet. The dent is meant to help the southerners differentiate the soup dumplings from other similar-looking buns, which do not contain soup. Apart from practical reasons, the varied appearances of dim sum snacks are also to provide variety and to enhance the dining experience of those who enjoy eating dim sum.

This cookbook compiles the recipes of some of the most popular dim sum snacks. It is a mix of traditional classics and new creative additions that will satisfy on all occasions. With illustrated instructions written in an easy-to-follow format, you can now discover the joy of preparing and enjoying dim sum in the comfort of your home.

COOKING TECHNIQUES

Steaming

Steaming is a healthy cooking technique, as oil is not essential when using this method to cook. In this technique, food is cooked by the heat from the steam of boiling water. A typical steamer has a separator to keep the food from coming into contact with the water below. It also comes with a lid, which covers the steamer during cooking so that the hot steam can properly cook the food. Steaming retains the shape and flavour of the food as it is a gentle cooking process. If a steamer is unavailable, a wok or pot with a metal frame can work just as well too. Fill the wok or pot with enough water and set a metal frame in the middle. Bring the water to a boil before lowering the food onto the metal frame to steam with the lid on.

Boiling

This method uses the heat from boiling water or other liquids to cook food. The liquid is brought to a boil before food is added to it for cooking. Boiling is also useful for softening ingredients, such as lotus leaves, as the leaves become more pliable, making it easier to fold over the ingredients for dishes like glutinous rice in lotus leaves. Vegetables are sometimes softened via boiling as an initial cooking process. This subsequently shortens the cooking time, be it for a stew or a pan-fried dish. Boiling food beforehand also prevents them from sticking to the frying pan during sautéing.

Pan-frying

As the name of this technique suggests, pan-frying is best done with a regular frying pan or sauté pan. The bottom of the pan should be evenly coated with oil, or the food will stick to the parts without oil, causing the food to burn easily. It will be harder to scrub off the burnt parts from the pan too. Some dim sum dishes, like bean curd rolls, are pan-fried prior to deep-frying, as this gives the rolls a crispier texture. Others, like the stuffed vegetables on page 69, are pan-fried until browned. This caramelisation process gives a fragrant taste to the food.

Deep-frying

Deep-frying is one of the common ways of preparing dim sum snacks. Contrary to popular belief, deep-fried food is not always soaked in oil, provided the oil temperature is just right. The food should be coated with a batter or crispy breading before deep-frying. This locks in moisture and acts as a seal against the oil. At the right temperature, the moisture from the food or batter will repel the oil and prevent it from seeping into the food. The optimum oil temperature for deep-frying is between 180–190°C (350–375°F), depending on the thickness and type of food. If a kitchen thermometer is unavailable, a simple test can be used to check the temperature. Insert a wooden chopstick into the heated oil. If bubbles form around the chopstick, the oil is ready for deep-frying. Another method is to drop a crumb of food into the hot oil, which is ready if the crumb floats and browns. Note that the pan or deep-fryer should not be overcrowded, as this can lower the oil temperature, which will affect the doneness of the food and cause it to absorb oil. Deep-fry in batches if necessary.

BASIC RECIPES

Seafood Paste

🦐 Makes about 320 g (11⅓ oz)

Prawns (shrimp) 300 g (10½ oz)

SEASONING

Salt 3 g (1/10 oz)

Chicken powder 3 g (1/10 oz)

Sugar 8 g (1/5 oz)

Potato starch 5 g (1/6 oz)

Oil 20 ml (2/3 fl oz)

Ground white pepper a dash

Sesame oil a dash

Note:
Seafood paste can be stored refrigerated for up to 3 days.

1 Using a blender, blend prawns into a paste.

2 Mix well with seasoning ingredients in a large bowl.

3 Use immediately. For more flavour, cover with cling film and leave to marinate overnight in the refrigerator before using.

Bun Pastry Dough

🌸 Makes about 250 g (9 oz)

Hong Kong flour 150 g (5$^1/_3$ oz)

Potato starch 10 g ($^1/_3$ oz)

Sugar 30 g (1 oz)

Yeast 2 g ($^1/_{15}$ oz)

Baking powder 2 g ($^1/_{15}$ oz)

Water 90–110 ml (3–3$^2/_3$ fl oz)

1 Combine all ingredients, except water, in a mixing bowl.

2 Make a well in the centre. Pour water into the well and mix until a smooth dough forms. Add more water if too dry. Dough is now ready for use.

Sweet Pastry Dough

🌸 Makes about 500 g (1 lb 1$^1/_2$ oz)

Wheat starch 60 g (2 oz)

Boiling water 60 ml (2 fl oz / $^1/_4$ cup)

Glutinous rice flour 150 g (5$^1/_3$ oz)

Sugar 60 g (2 oz)

Water about 130 ml (4$^2/_5$ fl oz)

Shortening 60 g (2 oz)

1 Pour wheat starch into a mixing bowl. Add boiling water and mix well. Set aside.

2 Pour glutinous rice flour and sugar into another mixing bowl. Make a well in the centre. Pour water into the well and stir to mix evenly. Combine with wheat starch batter and knead to mix evenly.

3 Add shortening and knead until dough is no longer sticky.

4 Cover with cling film and chill in the refrigerator for at least 20 minutes before using. This will prevent the pastry from being too sticky during wrapping.

DUMPLINGS

and

ROLLS

It takes some practice to get the correct texture and thickness for the skin, which should be thin enough such that it is not too chewy or doughy, but thick enough so that it doesn't break easily when held by chopsticks.

Har Kow Xia Jiao

🌸 Makes about 40 pieces

Seafood paste (see page 12) 320 g (11 1/3 oz)

HAR KOW SKIN

Wheat starch 200 g (7 oz)

Boiling water 300 ml (10 fl oz / 1 1/4 cups)

Potato starch 80 g (2 4/5 oz)

Shortening or vegetable oil about 1/4 tsp

1 Prepare har kow skin. Pour wheat starch into a mixing bowl. Add boiling water and stir with a spatula to mix.

2 Add potato starch and apply shortening or vegetable oil over the surface. Mix well until a smooth dough forms. Cover with cling film until ready to use to prevent the dough from drying out.

3 Roll dough into a long cylinder about 1.5–2 cm (3/4–4/5 in) in diameter. Cut out smaller pieces, each of about 1.5–2 cm (3/4–4/5 in) long.

4 Using the back of a knife, flatten each dough piece into a thin round sheet.

5 Scoop 1 tsp seafood paste onto the centre of a dough round. Pleat the edges to seal the dumpling. Repeat until all ingredients are used up.

6 Steam for 4 minutes over high heat.

7 Serve immediately.

Spicy Sour Wonton Hong You Chao Shou

✿ Makes about 30 pieces

White square wonton skin 30 sheets

SPICY SOUR SAUCE

Cooking oil 50 ml ($1^2/_3$ fl oz)

Chilli oil 35 ml ($1^1/_5$ fl oz)

Minced garlic 35 g ($1^1/_4$ oz)

Minced shallots 35 g ($1^1/_4$ oz)

Sugar 100 g ($3^1/_2$ oz)

Chicken powder 12 g ($^1/_3$ oz)

Salt 6 g ($^1/_5$ oz)

White vinegar 110 ml ($3^2/_3$ fl oz)

Spicy broad bean paste 150 ml (5 fl oz)

Seafood (hoisin) sauce 150 ml (5 fl oz)

FILLING

Prawns (shrimp) 100 g ($3^1/_2$ oz)

Potato starch 2 g ($^1/_{15}$ oz)

Salt 1 g ($^1/_{30}$ oz)

Chicken powder 1 g ($^1/_{30}$ oz)

Sugar 3 g ($^1/_{10}$ oz)

Ground white pepper a dash

Sesame oil a dash

Cooking oil a dash

1 Prepare spicy sour sauce. Heat cooking oil in a wok. Add chilli oil, garlic and shallots. Fry until fragrant.

2 Add the rest of the spicy sour sauce ingredients and bring to a boil. Remove from heat and keep warm.

3 Mix filling ingredients together in a bowl.

4 Lay a sheet of wonton skin on a clean flat surface such that the pointed tip is facing you. Spoon filling at the centre of the wonton skin. Wrap the bottom tip over the filling and roll it up halfway.

5 Fold one of the side flaps over the filling, pressing gently to secure the fold.

6 Cook wonton in boiling water until they float and the prawns look pink underneath the wonton skin.

7 Drain off water and dish out.

8 Pour spicy sour sauce over the wonton.

9 Garnish as desired and serve immediately.

A variant of prawn dumplings, this version has a spicy kick that adds flavour to wonton that is boiled instead of deep-fried.

A classic dim sum snack, *siew mai*, or pork dumplings, are generously packed with meat, prawns and mushrooms. Best enjoyed piping hot and straight from the steamer basket.

Siew Mai Shao Mai

❀ Makes about 40 pieces

Siew mai skin about 40 pieces

Prawn roe (ebiko) for garnishing

FILLING

Minced pork 300 g (10¹/₂ oz)

Prawn (shrimp) 200 g (7 oz)

Chinese mushrooms 50 g (1²/₃ oz)

Minced pork fat 50 g (1²/₃ oz)

SEASONING

Chicken powder 6 g (¹/₅ oz)

Salt 6 g (¹/₅ oz)

Sugar 15 g (¹/₂ oz)

Potato starch 15 g (¹/₂ oz)

Cooking oil 10 g (¹/₃ oz)

Ground white pepper a dash

Sesame oil a dash

1 Mix all ingredients for filling. Add all seasoning ingredients and mix well. Cover with cling film and leave to marinate for at least 10 minutes in the refrigerator.

2 Scoop filling onto siew mai skin, leaving a 0.5-cm (¹/₄-in) margin all around.

3 Form a circle with your thumb and forefinger. Place the siew mai skin with filling on top of the circle and gently push downwards until the skin wraps around the filling in a cylindrical shape. Gently flatten the top to compact the filling. Repeat until all ingredients are used up.

4 Grease the base of the steamer or line the bottom with steamer paper. Place siew mai onto the steamer and steam for 7 minutes over high heat.

5 Garnish with prawn roe and serve immediately.

Soup Dumplings Xiao Long Bao

🌸 Makes about 30 pieces

Carrot 1, peeled and sliced into thin rounds

Chopped spring onion (scallion) 10 g
(^{1}/$_2$ oz)

Cooking oil 1 Tbsp

GELATIN MIXTURE

Concentrated chicken stock 20 ml
(^{2}/$_3$ fl oz)

Boiling water 300 ml (10 fl oz / 1^1/$_4$ cups)

Gelatin powder 20 g (^{2}/$_3$ oz)

MEAT FILLING

Minced pork 300 g (10^1/$_2$ oz)

Oyster sauce 1 tsp

Potato starch 5 g (^{1}/$_6$ oz)

Salt a pinch

Chicken powder 3 g (^{1}/$_{10}$ oz)

Sugar 10 g (^{1}/$_3$ oz)

Sesame oil a dash

Ground white pepper a dash

Ginger juice ^{1}/$_2$ tsp

DOUGH

Hong Kong flour 100 g (3^1/$_2$ oz)

Bread flour 100 g (3^1/$_2$ oz)

Potato starch 100 g (3^1/$_2$ oz)

Salt a dash

Cooking oil a dash

Water 100 ml (3^1/$_3$ fl oz)

1 Prepare gelatin mixture. Mix stock with water in a saucepan. Add gelatin powder and bring to a boil. Set aside to cool.

2 In a mixing bowl, mix all ingredients for meat filling. Cover with cling film and leave to marinate for about 1 hour in the refrigerator.

3 Meanwhile, blanch carrot rounds in boiling water. Set aside.

4 Add gelatin mixture to meat filling. Mix in spring onion and oil. Set aside.

5 Combine dough ingredients. Mix well until a smooth dough is formed.

6 On a floured surface, roll dough into a long cylinder. Cut dough into 30 equal pieces. Using a rolling pin, roll out each piece into thin dough rounds.

7 Spoon combined meat and gelatin filling onto each dough round. Pleat to seal up filling. Repeat until all ingredients are used up.

8 Arrange carrot rounds onto steamer. Place a dumpling on top of each carrot round. Steam for 5 minutes over high heat. Serve immediately.

This is a version of soup dumplings from the southern Chinese. Unlike soup dumplings from the northern parts, the pleats are less defined and there is not as much soup within these dumplings.

The method for making blossom dumplings is similar to preparing *har kow*. Made to mimic flower blossoms, these savoury seafood dumplings look as good as they taste.

Blossom Dumplings Mei Hua Jiao

🌸 Makes about 40 pieces

Seafood paste (see page 12) 320 g (11¹/₃ oz)

Frozen mixed vegetables (peas, corn kernels and carrots) for garnishing

BLOSSOM DUMPLING SKIN

Wheat starch 200 g (7 oz)

Potato starch 80 g (2⁴/₅ oz)

Boiling water 200 ml (10 fl oz / 1¹/₄ cups)

Shortening or vegetable oil about ¹/₄ tsp

1 Prepare the skin. Pour wheat starch into a mixing bowl. Add boiling water and stir with a spatula to mix.

2 Add potato starch and apply shortening or vegetable oil over the surface. Mix well until a smooth dough forms. Cover with cling film until ready to use to prevent the dough from drying out.

3 Roll dough into a long cylinder about 1.5–2 cm (³/₄–⁴/₅ in) in diameter. Cut out smaller pieces, each of about 1.5–2 cm (³/₄–⁴/₅ in) long.

4 Using the back of a knife, flatten each dough piece into a thin round sheet.

5 Scoop 1 tsp seafood paste onto the centre of a dough round. Fold the dough round over the seafood paste until the top resembles a three-pointed star. The top should be sealed, with three flaps extending at the sides.

6 Take the tip of one flap and curve it towards the next flap, lightly pinching to join the tip to the centre of the star. Repeat until three round pleats are formed.

7 Place mixed vegetables into the pleats and steam for 4 minutes over high heat.

8 Serve immediately.

Deep-fried Wafer Rolls with Prawns and Mango Mang Guo Zha Xia Juan

🌸 Makes about 15 pieces

Prawns (shrimp) 300 g (10 ¹/₂ oz)

Ripe mango 1, peeled

Wafer papers about 40 sheets

Potato starch for coating

SEASONING

Salt 3 g (¹/₁₀ oz)

Sugar 8 g (¹/₅ oz)

Chicken powder 3 g (¹/₁₀ oz)

Potato starch 5 g (¹/₆ oz)

Coriander (cilantro) 10 g (¹/₃ oz)

Cooking oil a dash

Sesame oil a dash

Ground white pepper a dash

1 Shell and de-vein prawns. Wash and drain well before chopping into smaller pieces.

2 Add seasoning ingredients and mix until sticky. Chill in the refrigerator until needed.

3 Slice mango into 5 x 1-cm (2 x ¹/₂-in) strips.

4 Lay two sheets of wafer paper on a clean flat surface. Spoon about 1 Tbsp seasoned prawn filling near the bottom of the wafer papers. Lay a strip of mango over the filling and roll it up like a spring roll. Repeat until all ingredients are used up.

5 Coat wafer rolls with potato starch and deep-fry until golden brown.

6 Serve immediately.

The sweet juicy flesh of mango blends well with the savoury prawn filling, and gives a refreshing taste to the dish.

The crispy exterior is
a good contrast to the
soft delicious filling
of well-marinated
seafood. These rolls
can be eaten as a
snack or as part of
a main meal
with rice.

Deep-fried Bean Curd Rolls with Prawns Hei Zou

🌸 Makes about 18 pieces

Bean curd sheet 1, large

FILLING

Prawns (shrimp) 300 g (10½ oz)

Squid paste 100 g (3½ oz)

Water chestnut 20 g (⅔ oz), peeled and diced

Carrot 10 g (⅓ oz), peeled and diced

Coriander (cilantro) 10 g (⅓ oz), chopped

SEASONING

Salt 2 g (1/15 oz)

Chicken powder 2 g (1/15 oz)

Sugar 7 g (1/5 oz)

Potato starch 7 g (1/5 oz)

Ground white pepper a dash

Sesame oil a dash

1 Cut bean curd sheet into smaller sheets, each about 20 x 15 cm (8 x 6 in). Set aside.

2 Prepare filling. Shell and de-vein prawns. Wash and drain well before processing into a paste in a blender. Mix in squid paste and seasoning ingredients.

3 Add the rest of the filling ingredients and mix well.

4 Lay a sheet of trimmed bean curd skin on a clean flat surface. Spoon filling along the lower edge of bean curd skin and roll up the filling into a long and slightly flattened cylinder. Repeat until all ingredients are used up. Steam for 7 minutes over high heat.

5 Cut each steamed roll into six equal pieces.

6 Coat each piece with potato starch and deep-fry until golden brown.

7 Serve immediately with sweet dark soy sauce.

Deep-fried Prawn Dumplings
Ming Xia Jiao

🌸 Makes about 20-25 pieces

Seafood paste (see page 12) 320 g
   (11¹/₃ oz)

Wonton skin 30 sheets

Cooking oil for deep-frying

Mayonnaise for garnishing

1 Spoon about 1 tsp seafood paste at the centre of a wonton skin. Fold wonton skin over the filling to get a triangle. Press gently to seal the opening. Pleat the edges, nipping each pleat to further seal the dumpling. Repeat until all ingredients are used up.

2 Heat oil in a wok. Deep-fry dumplings until golden brown.

3 Garnish with mayonnaise and serve immediately.

Similar to deep-fried wonton, these dumplings get a western touch with a garnishing of mayonnaise, which also makes a pleasant dip for these deep-fried snacks.

This is a unique dumpling as it combines a dough that is slightly sweet and crispy with a savoury meat filling.

Sweet and Savoury Dumplings

Xian Shui Jiao

🌸 Makes about 25 dumplings

Sweet pastry dough (see page 13) 500 g (1 lb 1¹/₂ oz)

Potato starch mixture 2 tsp potato starch + 4 tsp water

Cooking oil for deep-frying

FILLING

Minced pork 100 g (3¹/₂ oz)

Chinese mushrooms 10 g (¹/₃ oz)

Salted vegetables 3 g (¹/₁₀ oz)

SEASONING

Minced garlic 1 tsp

Chicken powder a pinch

Sesame oil a dash

Sugar a pinch

Salt a pinch

Ground white pepper a dash

Note:
Deep-fry dumplings in batches so that the oil temperature stays constant. If the wok is overcrowded, the oil temperature will drop and the dumplings will absorb excess oil during cooking.

1 Blanch filling ingredients in boiling water. Drain and pat dry. Mix in seasoning ingredients, then thicken with potato starch mixture. Cover with cling film and leave to cool. Refrigerate for 1–2 hours.

2 On a floured surface, roll dough into a long cylinder. Cut dough into equal pieces, each about 20 g (²/₃ oz). Lightly flatten each piece into a 0.5 cm (¹/₄ in) thick round disc.

3 Scoop a small dollop of filling onto the centre of each dough round. Seal the filling and mould into a rugby ball shape.

4 Heat oil in a wok over high heat. Insert a wooden chopstick into the oil to test its temperature. Oil is ready for deep-frying when bubbles form round the chopstick. Turn off heat before adding dumplings into the oil, otherwise, the heavy dumplings will sink to the bottom and get burnt from the high heat. Use chopsticks to stir occasionally to prevent dumplings from sticking together.

5 When dumplings start to float, turn on to high heat again and deep-fry until golden brown. This will force out excess oil that was absorbed during the initial frying.

6 Serve immediately.

Deep-fried Wonton Zha Yun Tun

🌸 Makes about 25 pieces

Prawns (shrimp) 300 g (10¹/₂ oz)

Spring roll wrappers about 50 sheets

Cooking oil for deep-frying

SEASONING

Salt 3 g (¹/₁₀ oz)

Chicken powder 3 g (¹/₁₀ oz)

Sugar 8 g (¹/₅ oz)

Potato starch 5 g (¹/₆ oz)

Ground white pepper a dash

Sesame oil a dash

Cooking oil a dash

1 Shell and de-vein prawns. Wash and drain well before chopping into smaller pieces.

2 Add seasoning ingredients and mix until sticky. Chill in the refrigerator until needed.

3 Lay a sheet of spring roll wrapper on a clean flat surface such that the pointed tip is facing you. Spoon seasoned prawn filling at the centre of the spring roll wrapper. Wrap the bottom tip over the filling and roll it up into a cylinder. Bring both ends together and cross them over each other. Repeat until all ingredients are used up.

4 Heat oil in a wok. Deep-fry wonton until golden brown.

5 Serve with mayonnaise and sweet chilli sauce.

A classic favourite, deep-fried wonton is not only found at dim sum eateries, but also at various places from small cafés to established restaurants.

Bean curd sheets are used as wrappers for many deep-fried dishes, as the pleasing result of a fragrant crispy skin goes with almost any kind of filling.

Deep-fried Bean Curd Rolls with Seaweed Zi Cai Fu Pi Juan

🌸 Makes about 35 pieces

Bean curd sheets 2, large

Seaweed strips for wrapping

Cooking oil for deep-frying

Flour mixture 2 tsp plain (all-purpose) flour + 2 tsp water

FILLING

Prawns (shrimp) 150 g (5^1/$_3$ oz)

Minced pork 300 g (10^1/$_2$ oz)

SEASONING

Salt 5 g (^{1}/$_6$ oz)

Chicken powder 5 g (^{1}/$_6$ oz)

Sugar 15 g (^{1}/$_2$ oz)

Potato starch 10 g (^{1}/$_3$ oz)

Ground white pepper a dash

Sesame oil a dash

Cooking oil a dash

1 Cut bean curd sheets into 10-cm (4-in) squares. Set aside.

2 Prepare filling. Shell and de-vein prawns. Wash and drain well before chopping into smaller pieces. Mix in minced pork.

3 Add seasoning ingredients to filling and mix well.

4 Lay a bean curd sheet on a clean flat surface. Spoon filling along the bottom edge of the bean curd sheet. Roll it up into a flat rectangular parcel. Dab flour mixture along the edges to seal it. Repeat until all ingredients are used up.

5 Wrap a strip of seaweed around the middle of each parcel.

6 Heat oil in a wok. Deep-fry bean curd rolls until golden brown.

7 Serve immediately.

Crispy Yam Dumplings Wu Kok

Makes about 18 pieces

Potato starch mixture 2 tsp potato starch
+ 4 tsp water

Cooking oil for frying

Prawn cracker sticks for garnishing

YAM DOUGH

Yam 200 g (7 oz), peeled

Wheat starch 110 g (4 oz)

Boiling water 70 ml (2²/₅ fl oz)

Salt 2 g (¹/₁₅ oz)

Chicken powder 3 g (¹/₁₀ oz)

Sugar 5 g (¹/₆ oz)

Five spice powder a dash

Sesame oil a dash

Shortening 90 g (3¹/₅ oz)

MEAT FILLING

Minced garlic 1 tsp

Minced pork 100 g (3¹/₂ oz), blanched

Chinese mushrooms 10 g (¹/₃ oz), blanched

Chicken powder a pinch

Sesame oil a dash

Sugar a pinch

Salt a dash

Ground white pepper a dash

1 Prepare yam dough. Slice yam and steam for about 45 minutes or until soft. Mash into a paste.

2 Pour 70 g (2¹/₂ oz) wheat starch into another mixing bowl. Add boilng water and mix until a smooth dough forms. Add to mashed yam and mix. Add remaining yam dough ingredients, except shortening and remaining wheat starch, and mix well.

3 Add shortening and mix until well incorporated. Add remaining wheat starch and knead until a smooth dough forms. Set aside.

4 Prepare meat filling. Heat cooking oil in a wok. Fry garlic until fragrant. Add blanched pork and mushrooms, followed by the rest of the meat filling ingredients. Fry until fragrant, then thicken with potato starch mixture. Set aside to cool, then cover with cling film and chill in the refrigerator for 20–30 minutes.

5 Divide yam dough into 18 equal pieces. Shape each piece to resemble a small bowl. Spoon filling into the dough and wrap to seal it. Shape into a ball and lightly dent the top. Repeat until all ingredients are used up.

6 Heat oil in a wok. Deep-fry yam dumplings until golden brown. Remove from heat and drain off oil.

7 Garnish with prawn cracker sticks and serve immediately.

Sweet mashed yam with moist meat filling, deep-fried to a crisp golden brown — a mouth-watering combination that is popular with the young and old.

A variant of deep-fried prawn dumplings, these snacks are shaped to resemble the interesting shape of a pomegranate.

Pomegranate-shaped Prawns Shi Liu Xia

🌸 Makes about 50 pieces

Spring roll wrappers 50

Flour mixture 2 tsp plain (all-purpose)
flour + 2 tsp water

Seaweed strips for wrapping

Cooking oil for deep-frying

FILLING

Prawns (shrimp) 350 g (12$\frac{1}{2}$ oz)

Squid paste 150 g (5$\frac{1}{3}$ oz)

Potato starch 10 g ($\frac{1}{3}$ oz)

SEASONING

Salt 3 g ($\frac{1}{10}$ oz)

Chicken powder 3 g ($\frac{1}{10}$ oz)

Sugar 5 g ($\frac{1}{6}$ oz)

Ground white pepper a dash

Sesame oil a dash

1 Preparing filling. Shell and de-vein prawns. Wash and drain well before processing into a paste in a blender.

2 Mix in squid paste. Add potato starch and mix until sticky.

3 Add seasoning ingredients and mix well.

4 Divide filling into 50 balls. Cook in boiling water until they float. Set aside to cool.

5 Place a ball of filling at the centre of a sheet of spring roll wrapper. Roll it up like a cylinder, with the filling in the middle. Seal the opening with flour mixture. Bunch both ends to resemble a wrapped candy. Secure each bunched end with a strip of seaweed, sealing the opening with flour mixture.

6 Heat oil in a wok. Deep-fry pomegranate prawns until golden brown.

7 Serve immediately with mayonnaise.

Crispy Bread Rolls Xiang Cui Tu Si

🌸 Makes about 6 rolls

Celery 1 stalk

Carrot 1, peeled

Prawns (shrimp) 150 g (5$^1/_3$ oz)

Squid paste 50 g (1$^1/_3$ oz)

Square bread slices 6

Cooking oil for deep-frying

SEASONING

Salt 1 g ($^1/_{30}$ oz)

Chicken powder 1 g ($^1/_{30}$ oz)

Sugar 2 g ($^1/_{15}$ oz)

Ground white pepper a dash

Sesame oil a dash

Potato starch 3 g ($^1/_{10}$ oz)

1 Trim celery and carrots into thin strips. Each strip should be the same length as the bread. Blanch celery and carrots in boiling water, then set aside to cool.

2 Shell and de-vein prawns. Wash and drain well before processing into a paste in a blender.

3 Mix squid paste with prawn paste, then add seasoning ingredients and mix well. Chill in the refrigerator.

4 Meanwhile, flatten bread slices with a rolling pin. Trim away the crust only on two opposite sides.

5 Place a slice of bread on a clean flat surface, with the trimmed side facing you. Spoon prawn and squid filling along the centre of the bread. Top with celery and carrot strips, then roll up into a cylinder. Repeat until all ingredients are used up.

6 Heat oil in a wok. Deep-fry bread rolls until golden brown.

7 Trim away the ends with the crust, then halve each roll by slicing at a 45-degree angle and serve immediately.

These fun and delightful bread rolls are a creative way of serving sandwiches. Deep-frying the rolls adds crispiness and flavour.

The rich and fragrant oyster sauce is the star of this dish.

Bean Curd Rolls with Oyster Sauce

Xian Zhu Juan

🌸 Makes about 25 pieces

Bean curd sheets 2, large

Carrot 20 g ($^2/_3$ oz), diced

Chopped spring onion (scallion) 20 g ($^2/_3$ oz)

Potato starch for dusting

Cooking oil for frying

FILLING

Minced pork 300 g (10$^1/_2$ oz)

Prawns (shrimps) 150 g (5$^1/_3$ oz), shelled, deveined and chopped into smaller pieces

SEASONING

Potato starch 10 g ($^1/_3$ oz)

Salt 5 g ($^1/_6$ oz)

Chicken powder 5 g ($^1/_6$ oz)

Sugar 15 g ($^1/_2$ oz)

Ground white pepper a dash

Sesame oil a dash

SAUCE

Cooking oil 1 Tbsp

Shredded ginger 5 g ($^1/_6$ oz)

Spring onion (scallion) 1 stalk, chopped

Salt a pinch

Chicken powder a pinch

Sugar a pinch

Sesame oil a dash

Oyster sauce a dash

Ground white pepper a dash

Water 60 ml (2 fl oz / $^1/_4$ cup)

Potato starch mixture 2 tsp potato starch + 4 tsp water

1 Cut bean curd sheets into 10-cm (4-in) squares. Set aside.

2 Mix seasoning with carrot and spring onion. Mix in filling ingredients.

3 Lay a sheet of trimmed bean curd skin on a clean flat surface. Spoon filling along the lower edge of bean curd skin. Fold the sides inwards before rolling up into a cylinder. Dust with potato starch to prevent sticking during deep-frying. Repeat until all ingredients are used up.

4 Heat oil in a wok. Deep-fry bean curd rolls until golden brown. Drain off oil and set aside.

5 Prepare sauce. Heat cooking oil in a wok. Fry ginger and spring onion until fragrant. Add the rest of the sauce ingredients, except potato starch mixture. Bring to a boil.

6 Stir in potato starch mixture and cook for 1 minute more.

7 Pour sauce over bean curd rolls.

8 Garnish as desired and serve immediately.

Mini Chicken Frank Rolls Zi Cai Ji Juan

✿ Makes about 30 pieces

Seaweed 1 large sheet, 20 x 30 cm
(8 x 12 in)

Chicken franks 10, cut into 3 sections

DOUGH

Hong Kong flour 150 g (5¹⁄₃ oz)

Baking powder 6 g (¹⁄₅ oz)

Sugar 55 g (2 oz)

Water 65 ml (2¹⁄₅ fl oz)

1 Prepare dough. Add all ingredients, except water, into a mixing bowl. Make a well in the centre. Pour water into the well and mix until a smooth dough forms.

2 On a floured surface, roll out dough into a 30 x 30-cm (12 x 12-in) sheet. Dough should be as thin as possible.

3 Dampen the surface of the dough sheet and apply a sheet of seaweed on top.

4 Roll up dough into a cylinder. The roll should not be too tight or too loose, and should have a diameter of about 4 cm (1³⁄₄ in). Cover with cling film and leave to chill in the refrigerator for about 10 minutes.

5 Cut chilled dough into thin oval sheets, each about 3 mm (¹⁄₈ in) thick. Do this by slicing at a 45-degree angle starting from one end of the dough.

6 Wrap a dough sheet around a piece of chicken frank. Repeat until all ingredients are used up.

7 Steam for 3–4 minutes over high heat.

8 Serve immediately.

These adorable mini rolls may look fancy, but they are not difficult to make at all.

This Shanghainese treat is a popular favourite. These meat buns are first steamed before pan-frying, giving them a soft pillowy texture and a slightly crisp crust.

Pan-fried Meat Buns Sheng Jian Bao

🌸 Makes about 25 pieces

Bun pastry dough (see page 13) 540 g
(1 lb 3 oz)

Chopped spring onion (scallion) 30 g (1 oz)

Cooking oil for pan-frying

FILLING

Cabbage 100 g (3^1/$_2$ oz), finely chopped

Minced pork 300 g (10^1/$_2$ oz)

SEASONING

Potato starch 5 g (^{1}/$_6$ oz)

Salt a pinch

Chicken powder 3 g (^{1}/$_{10}$ oz)

Sugar 10 g (^{1}/$_3$ oz)

Oil a dash

Sesame oil a dash

Ground white pepper a dash

Ginger juice a dash

1 Prepare filling. Blanch cabbage in boiling water. Drain and set aside.

2 Add seasoning ingredients to minced pork and mix well. Mix in blanched cabbage. Cover with cling film and chill in the refrigerator for 20–30 minutes.

3 On a floured surface, roll dough into a long cylinder. Divide dough into 25 equal pieces.

4 Lightly flatten each piece into a flat round disc. Spoon filling into dough round and form pleats at the top to seal it.

5 Dampen the tops of the buns and coat with spring onions.

6 Leave buns to prove for 45 minutes.

7 Steam buns for 4 minutes over high heat.

8 Heat oil in a wok. Pan-fry buns until golden brown.

9 Serve immediately.

Chives Dumplings Jiu Cai Jiao Zi

🌸 Makes about 35 pieces

Chives 100 g (3^1/$_2$ oz), chopped

Cooking oil 1 Tbsp

FILLING

Minced pork 300 g (10^1/$_2$ oz)

Salt 2 g (^{1}/$_{15}$ oz)

Chicken powder 2 g (^{1}/$_{15}$ oz)

Sugar 10 g (^{1}/$_3$ oz)

Potato starch 5 g (^{1}/$_6$ oz)

Ground white pepper a dash

Sesame oil a dash

Ginger juice a dash

PASTRY

Hong Kong flour 200 g (7 oz)

Bread flour 50 g (1^2/$_3$ oz)

Water 130 ml (4^2/$_5$ fl oz)

Cooking oil a dash

Salt a pinch

1   Mix filling ingredients in a large mixing bowl. Mix in chopped chives, cover with cling film and refrigerate for 20–30 minutes.

2   Mix pastry ingredients together until a smooth dough forms.

3   On a floured surface, roll dough into a long cylinder. Divide dough into 35 equal pieces.

4   Lightly flatten each piece into a flat round disc. Spoon filling into dough round and form pleats at the top to seal it.

5   Heat oil in a pan. Arrange each dumpling to sit nicely on its flat side in the pan. Leave dumplings to pan-fry until the bases have browned.

6   Add water until it is about 1 cm (^{1}/$_2$ in) high. Cover and leave dumplings to cook over high heat until water has almost evaporated.

7   Serve immediately.

Prior to steaming, these dumplings are pan-fried until the bases are browned and stuck to the pan, thus their Chinese name *guo tie*, which literally means "sticking to the pan".

SMALL DISHES

Steamed Fish Head with Fermented Black Beans Dou Chi Zheng Yu

Serves 4–5

Fish head 1, about 600 g (1 lb 5²/₅ oz)

Fermented black beans 1 heaped Tbsp

Potato starch 10 g (¹/₃ oz)

Shredded ginger 10 g (¹/₃ oz)

Shredded spring onion (scallion) for garnishing

Shredded red chilli for garnishing

SEASONING

Chu hou sauce 20 g (²/₃ oz)

Guilin chilli sauce 20 g (²/₃ oz)

Oyster sauce 1¹/₂ Tbsp

Seafood (hoisin) sauce 1¹/₂ Tbsp

Chicken powder 7 g (¹/₅ oz)

Salt 7 g (¹/₅ oz)

Sugar 16 g (¹/₂ oz)

Ginger juice a dash

Ground black pepper a dash

Ground white pepper a dash

Sesame oil a dash

Cooking oil a dash

1 Cut fish head into bite-size pieces. Rinse and drain.

2 Blanch fermented black beans in boiling water. Drain and pan-fry until fragrant. Set aside.

3 Coat fish head pieces evenly with potato starch.

4 Add all seasoning ingredients to fish head pieces and mix evenly.

5 Steam for 15 minutes.

6 Garnish with spring onion and red chilli before serving.

Fish head is typical food on a Chinese dining table. The myriad of spices and seasoning ingredients removes any trace of fishiness, and makes this a satisfying dish.

Phoenix claws is an elegant name for these fragrant chicken feet, which is very popular in Chinese cuisine.

Phoenix Claws Feng Zhao

🌸 Serves 5–6

Chicken claws 600 g (1 lb 5²/₅ oz)

Vinegar 1 tsp

Maltose 1 tsp

Cooking oil for deep-frying

Spring onion (scallion) 1 stalk, cut into 5-cm (2-in) lengths

Star anise 5

Szechuan peppercorns 3 g (¹/₁₀ oz)

Ginger slices 30 g (1 oz)

Potato starch 20 g (²/₃ oz)

Red chillies 3, de-seeded and sliced

SEASONING

Salt 1 tsp

Chicken powder 1 tsp

Sugar 1 tsp

Ground white pepper a dash

Sesame oil a dash

SAUCE

Minced garlic 20 g (²/₃ oz)

Fermented black beans 1 Tbsp, rinsed

Char siew sauce 2 tsp

Guilin chilli sauce 1 tsp

Chu hou sauce 1 tsp

Seafood (hoisin) sauce 2 tsp

Salt 5 g (¹/₆ oz)

Chicken powder 5 g (¹/₆ oz)

Ground white pepper a dash

Sesame oil a dash

Cooking oil a dash

1 Wash chicken claws and cut off nails from the tips, then halve each claw.

2 Coat chicken claws evenly with vinegar and maltose. Blanch in boiling water, then set aside.

3 Heat oil in a wok. Deep-fry chicken claws over high heat until golden brown. Remove from heat and place chicken claws into a mixing bowl. Mix seasoning ingredients with chicken claws.

4 Add spring onion, star anise, Szechuan peppercorns and ginger slices. Pour in just enough water to cover chicken claws. Boil or steam for 45 minutes over medium heat.

5 Meanwhile, prepare sauce ingredients. Fry half of the garlic until browned and fragrant. Mix with raw garlic and set aside. Fry fermented black beans until fragrant and set aside.

6 Rinse chicken claws under cold running water. Drain and coat evenly with potato starch.

7 Mix all sauce ingredients together. Pour the sauce over coated chicken claws and steam for 5 minutes over medium heat.

8 Garnish with chilli slices and serve immediately.

Steamed Pork Ribs with Fermented Black Beans Dou Chi Zheng Pai Gu

🌸 Serves 5–6

Pork ribs 600 g (1 lb 5²/₅ oz)

Potato starch 20 g (²/₃ oz)

Minced garlic 20 g (²/₃ oz)

Fermented black beans 1 Tbsp, rinsed

Pickled plum 1, de-seeded and chopped

Sesame oil a dash

Ground white pepper a dash

Red chilli 1, de-seeded and sliced

SEASONING

Potato starch 10 g (¹/₃ oz)

Salt 6 g (¹/₅ oz)

Chicken powder 6 g (¹/₅ oz)

Sugar 16 g (¹/₂ oz)

1 Cut pork ribs into bite-size pieces.

2 Marinate pork ribs with potato starch for about half an hour.

3 Meanwhile, fry half of the garlic until browned and fragrant. Mix with raw garlic and set aside.

4 Fry fermented black beans until fragrant. Set aside.

5 Rinse marinated pork ribs under running water and drain well.

6 Add seasoning ingredients and mix well.

7 Mix in remaining ingredients, except chilli slices, and steam for 8 minutes over medium heat.

8 Garnish with chilli slices and serve immediately.

Leave some fat on the pork ribs, as this will give a smoother texture to the cooked meat. This dish goes very well with steamed rice.

Some people enjoy chewing on the sugarcane sticks after they finish eating the seafood filling, as the sweet juice from the sugarcane is simply hard to resist!

Vietnamese Sugarcane Prawns
Yue Nan Zhe Xia

🌸 Makes about 20–25 pieces

Sugarcane 2 stalks, each about 15 cm (6 in) long

Breadcrumbs 300 g (10½ oz)

Cooking oil for deep-frying

FILLING

Prawns (shrimp) 300 g (10½ oz)

Squid paste 150 g (5⅓ oz)

SEASONING

Salt 2 g (¹/₁₅ oz)

Chicken powder 2 g (¹/₁₅ oz)

Sugar 4 g (¹/₇ oz)

Potato starch 5 g (¹/₆ oz)

Ground white pepper a dash

Sesame oil a dash

Note:
The filling can be kept in the refrigerator for up to 3 days, and up to 2 weeks in the freezer.

1 Trim off the tough outer stem of the sugarcane stalks.

2 Cut each stalk into 1-cm (½-in) strips.

3 Prepare filling. Shell and de-vein prawns. Wash and drain well before processing into a paste in a blender. Mix in squid paste and seasoning ingredients.

4 Dampen hands and gather filling to wrap around each sugarcane strip. Coat evenly with breadcrumbs. Repeat until all ingredients are used up.

5 Heat oil in a wok and deep-fry until golden brown.

6 Serve immediately with sweet chilli sauce.

Lemongrass Sticks Xiang Mao Chuan

🌸 Makes about 25 pieces

Lemongrass 6 stalks

Cooking oil for deep-frying

FILLING

Prawns (shrimp) 200 g (7 oz)

Minced pork 200 g (7 oz)

Squid paste 200 g (7 oz)

Water chestnut 50 g ($1^2/_3$ oz), peeled and diced

Chopped spring onion (scallion) 15 g ($^1/_2$ oz)

Carrot 15 g ($^1/_2$ oz), peeled and diced

SEASONING

Potato starch 10 g ($^1/_3$ oz)

Salt 7 g ($^1/_5$ oz)

Chicken powder 7 g ($^1/_5$ oz)

Sugar 15 g ($^1/_2$ oz)

Cooking oil 10 ml ($^1/_3$ fl oz)

Five spice powder a dash

Sesame oil a dash

1 Prepare filling. Shell and de-vein prawns. Wash and drain well before processing into a paste in a blender.

2 Add minced pork and mix well, then mix in squid paste. Mix until a sticky paste is formed.

3 Mix in remaining filling ingredients.

4 Add seasoning ingredients and mix well. Set aside.

5 Trim away the lower bulb of each lemongrass stalk, then cut into 6-cm ($2^1/_2$-in) long strips.

6 With a spoon ready in one hand, dampen the other hand with some water. Use the damp hand to gather some filling and lightly squeeze out a ball of filling. Scoop the ball of filling with the spoon and set it aside. Repeat until filling is used up.

7 Wrap each ball of filling around a lemongrass strip, leaving half of the strip exposed. Repeat until all ingredients are used up.

8 Heat oil in a wok. Deep-fry lemongrass sticks until golden brown.

9 Serve immediately.

Infused with the subtle citrus flavour of lemongrass, this aromatic blend of meat and seafood is an appetising snack.

These are open-face sandwiches that have been deep-fried to golden brown perfection. They are addictive snacks that also make very good appetisers.

Mini Salmon Toast San Wen Yu Tu Si

🌸 Makes about 40 pieces

Square bread slices 10

Black sesame seeds 20 g ($^2/_3$ oz)

White sesame seeds 150 g ($5^1/_3$ oz)

Cooking oil for deep-frying

FILLING

Salmon 100 g ($3^1/_2$ oz), minced

Squid paste 200 g (7 oz)

Diced onion 15 g ($^1/_2$ oz)

Diced celery 15 g ($^1/_2$ oz)

SEASONING

Potato starch 4 g ($^1/_7$ oz)

Salt 1 g ($^1/_{30}$ oz)

Chicken powder 1 g ($^1/_{30}$ oz)

Sugar 4 g ($^1/_7$ oz)

Ground white pepper a dash

Sesame oil a dash

1 Prepare filling. Mix salmon and squid paste together. Add seasoning ingredients and mix evenly.

2 Mix in diced onion and celery. Set aside.

3 Using a round cutter, cut out rounds from bread slices.

4 Spoon filling onto each bread round.

5 Mix black and white sesame seeds together. Lightly dampen filing and coat with sesame seeds.

6 Heat oil in a wok. Deep-fry salmon toast until golden brown.

7 Serve immediately.

Paper-wrapped Chicken Zhi Bao Ji

🌸 Makes 12–15 packets

Chicken thigh 300 g (10$^{1}/_{2}$ oz)

Paper wrappers 15 packets

Flour mixture 2 tsp plain (all-purpose) flour + 2 tsp water

Cooking oil for deep-frying

SEASONING

Salt 2 g ($^{1}/_{15}$ oz)

Chicken powder 2 g ($^{1}/_{15}$ oz)

Sugar 4 g ($^{1}/_{7}$ oz)

Sesame oil 3 ml ($^{1}/_{10}$ fl oz)

Oyster sauce 1 tsp

Dark soy sauce 3 ml ($^{1}/_{10}$ fl oz)

Minced garlic 6 g ($^{1}/_{5}$ oz)

Ginger juice 10 ml ($^{1}/_{3}$ fl oz)

Rice wine 10 ml ($^{1}/_{3}$ fl oz)

Ground white pepper a dash

Five spice powder a dash

1 Cut chicken thigh into smaller pieces.

2 Mix all seasoning ingredients together and use the mixture to marinate chicken pieces.

3 Pack chicken pieces into paper wrappers. Fold the open edges down and seal with flour mixture.

4 Heat oil in a wok. Deep-fry paper-wrapped chicken until golden brown.

5 Serve immediately.

While this dish may be a little messy to eat, it is hard to resist tasty chicken thigh meat that is marinated with a good number of spices.

This is actually yong tau foo served with a savoury sauce. In Chinese, niang means "stuffed", and san bao means "three treasures", referring to the eggplant, red chilli, and capsicum.

Stuffed Vegetables Niang San Bao

🌸 Makes about 35 pieces

Eggplant (aubergine/brinjal) 1, cut into 1 cm ($^1/_2$ in) thick rounds

Red chillies 3

Capsicum (bell pepper) 1

Potato starch for coating

Cooking oil for pan-frying

FILLING

Prawns (shrimps) 200 g (7 oz)

Squid paste 100 g (3$^1/_2$ oz)

Salt 2 g ($^1/_{15}$ oz)

Potato starch 4 g ($^1/_7$ oz)

Chicken powder a pinch

Sugar 6 g ($^1/_5$ oz)

Ground white pepper a dash

Sesame oil a dash

SAUCE

Salt a pinch

Chicken powder a pinch

Sugar a pinch

Black soy sauce a dash

Oyster sauce a dash

Minced garlic 1 tsp

Potato starch a pinch

1 Butterfly each eggplant round.

2 Slit chillies lengthwise to de-seed, then halve them horizontally.

3 Cut capsicum in half and remove the core. Cut each half into quarters.

4 Coat the insides of the vegetables with potato starch.

5 Prepare filling. Shell and de-vein prawns. Wash and drain well before chopping into smaller pieces.

6 Mix in seasoning ingredients, followed by squid paste. Stir until mixture is sticky. Apply filling onto vegetables.

7 Heat a pan for about 1 minute. Add 2 Tbsp oil and arrange stuffed vegetables, filling side down, to pan-fry for about 1 minute.

8 Ladle in about 125 ml (4 fl oz / $^1/_2$ cup) water and cover with a lid. Cook for about 4 minutes more.

9 Meanwhile, mix sauce ingredients together. Dish out stuffed vegetables and serve with the sauce.

RICE and
SAVOURY CAKES

Glutinous Rice in Lotus Leaf He Ye Fan

❀ Makes about 16 parcels

Lotus leaves 4

Glutinous rice 600 g (1 lb 5²/₅ oz), washed

Water about 400 ml (13¹/₂ fl oz)

Cooking oil for pan-frying

Chinese sausage 80 g (2⁴/₅ oz)

Dried shrimps 80 g (2⁴/₅ oz)

Chinese mushrooms 40 g (1¹/₃ oz)

Braised peanuts 1 can, about 170 g (6 oz)

Chopped spring onion (scallion) 30 g (1 oz)

Fried shallots 30 g (1 oz) + more for garnishing

SEASONING

Salt 9 g (¹/₃ oz)

Chicken powder 9 g (¹/₃ oz)

Sugar 25 g (⁴/₅ oz)

Ground white pepper a dash

Sesame oil a dash

Dark soy sauce a dash

Boiling water 150 ml (5 fl oz)

Note:
If you do not wish to cook all the portions at one go, the remainder can be stored in the freezer for 1–2 weeks.

1 Cut off the tough base of each lotus leaf. Trim away the rough edges and halve it. Cut each leaf into four equal portions.

2 Blanch lotus leaves in boiling water. Set aside to cool.

3 Add water to glutinous rice. The water level should be about the same height as the glutinous rice. Steam for 45 minutes.

4 Meanwhile, heat oil in a wok. Pan-fry sausage, dried shrimps and mushrooms until fragrant. Add braised peanuts and stir to mix briefly. Remove from heat and add to steamed glutinous rice.

5 Add seasoning ingredients to glutinous rice mixture and mix well.

6 Stir in spring onion and fried shallots. Divide into 16 portions.

7 Place each portion onto the centre of a sheet of lotus leaf. Bring both sides of the lotus leaf over the glutinous rice mixture, then roll up into a rectangular parcel. Repeat until all parcels are wrapped.

8 Steam for 5 minutes over medium heat.

9 Serve immediately.

The lotus leaf imparts an aromatic fragrance to the filling.

Usually served in squares, this popular breakfast food gets a modern twist here as it is served in mini bowls. The defining features of this yam cake are its garnishing and sauce, which are always part of the dish.

Yam Cake Yu Tou Gao

🌸 Makes about 20 small cakes

Yam 1, peeled

Cooking oil for deep-frying and pan-frying

Boiling water 800 ml (27 fl oz)

BATTER

Rice flour 150 g (5$^{1}/_{3}$ oz)

Wheat starch 35 g (1$^{1}/_{4}$ oz)

Potato starch 35 g (1$^{1}/_{4}$ oz)

Salt 10 g ($^{1}/_{3}$ oz)

Chicken powder 10 g ($^{1}/_{3}$ oz)

Sugar 35 g (1$^{1}/_{4}$ oz)

Water 600 ml (19 fl oz)

Pepper a dash

Sesame oil a dash

Cooking oil a dash

GARNISHING

Dried shimps 40 g (1$^{1}/_{3}$ oz), chopped

Chinese sausage 40 g (1$^{1}/_{3}$ oz), chopped

Fried shallots 20 g ($^{2}/_{3}$ oz)

Chopped spring onion (scallion) 20 g ($^{2}/_{3}$ oz)

SAUCE

Light soy sauce 100 ml (3$^{1}/_{3}$ fl oz)

Dark soy sauce 10 ml ($^{1}/_{3}$ fl oz)

Chicken powder 12 g ($^{1}/_{3}$ oz)

Sugar 50 g (1$^{2}/_{3}$ oz)

Water 300 ml (10 fl oz / 1$^{1}/_{4}$ cups)

1 Dice yam into small cubes. Deep-fry yam cubes until browned and set aside.

2 Combine batter ingredients in a mixing bowl. Stir in boiling water and mix well. Ladle into individual serving bowls or into one large tray. Steam for 40 minutes over high heat.

3 Meanwhile, prepare garnishing. Heat oil in a wok. Pan-fry dried shimps and sausage until fragrant. Remove from heat, then mix in fried shallots and spring onion. Set aside.

4 Mix all ingredients for the sauce.

5 When yam cake is ready, top with garnishing and spoon sauce over it. Serve immediately.

Pan-fried Carrot Cake Luo Bo Gao

🌸 Serves 3–4

Cooking oil for frying

Dried shrimps 20 g (²/₃ oz), rinsed, soaked and chopped

Chinese sausage 20 g (²/₃ oz), chopped

Radish 100 g (3¹/₂ oz), peeled and shredded

Water 500 ml (16 fl oz / 2 cups)

BATTER

Rice flour 160 g (5²/₃ oz)

Potato starch 20 g (²/₃ oz)

Wheat starch 20 g (²/₃ oz)

Sugar 20 g (²/₃ oz)

Chicken powder 6 g (¹/₅ oz)

Salt 4 g (¹/₇ oz)

Water 200 ml (6³/₄ fl oz)

Ground white pepper a dash

Sesame oil a dash

1 Mix batter ingredients together. Stir well and set aside.

2 Heat oil in a wok. Fry shrimps, sausage and radish until fragrant.

3 Bring 500 ml (16 fl oz / 2 cups) water to a boil. Add in fried ingredients. Add this mixture to the batter and stir to mix well.

4 Transfer batter to a tray and steam for 35 minutes over high heat.

5 Leave to cool and refrigerate overnight.

6 Heat oil in a wok. Pan-fry until browned.

7 Serve immediately with chilli sauce.

Somewhat of a misnomer, the classic carrot cake is actually flavoured by radish. Radish and carrot are both called *luo bo* in Mandarin, which most probably led to this dish being named as such.

Well seasoned and fragrant, this hearty snack is a favourite among dim sum lovers. Because it is filling, most people share a serving among a few persons so that they are not too full to enjoy other dim sum snacks.

Steamed Chicken Glutinous Rice

Lor Mai Kai

🌸 Makes about 15 portions

Glutinous rice 600 g (1 lb 5²/₅ oz)

Water 400 ml (13¹/₂ fl oz)

Boneless chicken thigh 300 g (10¹/₂ oz),
cut into bite-size pieces

SEASONING

Chicken powder 6 g (¹/₅ oz)

Salt 6 g (¹/₅ oz)

Sugar 30 g (1 oz)

Oyster sauce 2 Tbsp

Boiling water 300 ml (10 fl oz /
1¹/₄ cups)

Sesame oil a dash

Cooking oil a dash

Ground white pepper a dash

Dark soy sauce a dash

MARINADE

Potato starch 6 g (¹/₅ oz)

Chicken powder 3 g (¹/₁₀ oz)

Salt 3 g (¹/₁₀ oz)

Sugar 8 g (¹/₅ oz)

Oyster sauce 1 tsp

Sesame oil a dash

Cooking oil a dash

Ground white pepper a dash

Dark soy sauce a dash

Note:
If you do not wish to cook all
the portions at one go, the
remainder can be stored in the
freezer for 1–2 weeks.

1 Steam glutinous rice with water for 45 minutes.
   Stir in seasoning ingredients and mix evenly.

2 Coat chicken pieces evenly with marinade
   ingredients. Arrange marinated chicken pieces
   at the bottom of each aluminium case. Top with
   glutinous rice until each case is full.

3 Steam for 20 minutes over medium heat.

4 Serve immediately.

Steamed Char Siew and Egg Rice

Fan Cai

🌸 Makes about 16 portions

Jasmine rice 800 g (1³/₄ lb), steamed with 800 ml (27 fl oz) water

Char siew 300 g (10¹/₂ oz)

Hardboiled eggs 3, peeled

SEASONING

Salt 12 g (¹/₃ oz)

Chicken powder 12 g (¹/₃ oz)

Sugar 20 g (²/₃ oz)

Oyster sauce 50 ml (1²/₃ fl oz)

Seafood (hoisin) sauce 50 ml (1²/₃ fl oz)

Char siew **sauce** 50 ml (1²/₃ fl oz)

Dark soy sauce 2 Tbsp

Sesame oil 10 ml (¹/₃ fl oz)

Pepper a dash

Boiling water 100 ml (3¹/₃ fl oz)

Note:
If you do not wish to cook all the portions at one go, the remainder can be stored in the freezer for 1–2 weeks.

1 Mix all seasoning ingredients together and add to steamed rice. Set aside.

2 Cut *char siew* into slices and cut the eggs into wedges.

3 Arrange *char siew* slices and egg wedges at the bottom of each aluminium foil case. Top with rice until each case is full.

4 Steam for 7 minutes over medium heat.

5 Serve immediately.

This savoury dish is slightly sweeter than *lor mai kai*, as the *char siew* sauce is the main seasoning ingredient. Like the *lor mai kai*, a serving of *fan cai* is usually shared among two to four persons.

PASTRIES
and DESSERTS

Glutinous Rice Balls with Grated Coconut Nuo Mi Ci

🌸 Makes about 25 rice balls

Sweet pastry dough (see page 13) 500 g
  (1 lb 1¹/₂ oz)

Red bean paste 200 g (7 oz)

Grated coconut 200 g (7 oz)

1 On a floured surface, roll dough into a long cylinder. Cut dough into equal pieces, each about 20 g (²/₃ oz). Lightly flatten each piece into a 0.5 cm (¹/₄ in) thick round disc.

2 Scoop a small dollop of red bean paste onto the centre of each dough round. Seal the red bean filling and mould into a round ball. Repeat until all ingredients are used up.

3 Steam for about 5 minutes over medium heat.

4 Coat evenly with grated coconut and serve immediately.

Coated with snowy white grated coconut, each of these glutinous rice balls is a generous filling of red bean paste encased in soft chewy dough.

This recipe uses a walnut-shaped mould and coffee-flavoured milk for a rich smooth taste. Choose a flavoured milk of your choice and mould each dumpling into any desired shape to create your own version of this delightful treat.

Snow Skin Dumplings Bing Pi Gao

🌸 Makes about 16 dumplings

Rice flour 75 g (2²/₃ oz)

Glutinous rice flour 45 g (1¹/₂ oz)

Wheat starch 30 g (1 oz)

Full cream milk of desired flavour 275 ml (9¹/₃ fl oz)

Sugar 75 g (2²/₃ oz)

Butter 30 g (1 oz)

FILLING

Lotus, red bean or green tea paste 200 g (7 oz)

1 Mix all ingredients, except the filling, in a mixing bowl. Stir to mix well. Cover and cook for 10 minutes over high heat, stirring every 2–3 minutes, until the dough is no longer watery.

2 Knead dough until smooth.

3 Roll dough into a long cylinder about 2 cm (⁴/₅ in) in diameter. Cut out smaller pieces, each of about 2 cm (⁴/₅ in) long.

4 Lightly flatten each piece into a 0.5 cm (¹/₄ in) thick round disc.

5 Scoop a small dollop of filling onto the centre of each dough round. Seal the filling and mould into desired shape. Repeat until all ingredients are used up.

6 Garnish as desired and serve immediately.

Sweet Potato Dumplings Hong Shu Gao

🌸 Makes about 30 pieces

Purple sweet potato 110 g (4 oz), peeled
and sliced

Wheat starch 100 g (3¹/₂ oz)

Boiling water 100 ml (3¹/₃ fl oz)

Sugar 20 g (²/₃ oz)

Butter 50 g (1²/₃ oz)

Green tea paste 200 g (7 oz)

1 Steam sweet potato slices until soft. Mash and
set aside.

2 Pour wheat starch into a mixing bowl and make a
well in the centre. Pour boiling water into the well
and stir to mix. Add mashed sweet potato and
knead to mix evenly.

3 Add sugar and butter. Knead until well
incorporated. Cover with cling film and leave to
chill in the refrigerator for 20–30 minutes.

4 Divide chilled dough into small dough rounds.
Flatten each round and place green tea paste in the
centre. Wrap dough around the green tea filling and
mould it into the shape of an eggplant.

5 Roll small strips of green tea paste. Gently adhere
two strips in a cross over the top of each eggplant to
complete the shape.

6 Steam for 3 minutes over high heat and serve
immediately.

Shape these dumplings as desired to create fancy snacks that will appeal to the young and old. Feel free to replace the green tea paste with other types of filling.

This is sold in many Chinese food eateries or snack stalls. The generous filling of lotus paste encased in a sweet crispy dough is made all the more fragrant with sesame seeds.

Deep-fried Glutinous Rice Balls Jian Dui

🌺 Makes about 25 balls

Sweet pastry dough (see page 13) 500 g
(1 lb 1¹/₂ oz)

Lotus paste 200 g (7 oz)

White sesame seeds 20 g (²/₃ oz)

Cooking oil for deep-frying

Note:
Deep-fry rice balls in batches so that the oil temperature stays constant. If the wok is overcrowded, the oil temperature will drop and the rice balls will absorb excess oil during cooking.

1 On a floured surface, roll dough into a long cylinder. Cut dough into equal pieces, each about 20 g (²/₃ oz). Lightly flatten each piece into a 0.5 cm (¹/₄ in) thick round disc.

2 Scoop a small dollop of lotus paste onto the centre of each dough round. Seal the lotus paste filling and mould into a round ball. Dampen it and coat all over with sesame seeds. Repeat until all ingredients are used up.

3 Heat oil in a wok over high heat. Insert a wooden chopstick into the oil to test its temperature. Oil is ready for deep-frying when bubbles form round the chopstick. Turn off heat before adding rice balls into the oil, otherwise, due to the heavy filling, they will sink to the bottom and get burnt from the high heat. Use chopsticks to stir occasionally to prevent them from sticking together.

4 When the rice balls start to float, turn on to high heat again and deep-fry until golden brown. This will force out excess oil that was absorbed during the initial frying.

5 Serve immediately.

Salted Egg Yolk Custard Buns Liu Sha Bao

✿ Makes about 20 small buns

Bun pastry dough (see page 13)
  250 g (9 oz)

CUSTARD FILLING

Salted egg yolks 70 g (2$^1/_2$ oz)

Castor sugar 140 g (5 oz)

Full cream milk 10 ml ($^1/_3$ fl oz)

Milk powder 50 g (1$^2/_3$ oz)

Custard powder 50 g (1$^2/_3$ oz)

Butter 90 g (3$^1/_5$ oz)

1 Prepare custard filling. Steam salted egg yolks over medium heat for about 5 minutes. Mash and add remaining ingredients for the filling. Mix well and chill in the freezer until it is of ice-cream consistency.

2 Roll dough into a long cylinder. Divide dough into 20 equal pieces. Lightly flatten each piece into a 0.5 cm ($^1/_4$ in) thick round disc.

3 Using a melon baller, scoop out balls of frozen custard filling.

4 Place each ball of custard filling onto the centre of a dough round. Seal filling and roll into a ball, then place into a mini tart tin lined with tart liner. Repeat until all ingredients are used up.

5 Leave buns to prove for 45 minutes.

6 Steam for 4 minutes over medium heat, opening the lid halfway through for a few seconds to release heat, or the dough may crack from the high heat, causing the custard to flow out.

7 Serve immediately.

This is a fairly modern addition to the dim sum menu, and is very popular because of the rich lava of salted egg yolk custard.

It's hard to resist the sweet custard filling nestled within a light crisp pastry. This is both a wonderful snack and a satisfying dessert.

Deep-fried Custard Buns Xiang Zha Nai Huang Bao

🌸 Makes about 25 buns

Bun pastry dough (see page 13)
    250 g (9 oz)

Cooking oil for deep-frying

CUSTARD

Eggs 3

Sugar 150 g (5¹/₃ oz)

Hong Kong flour 35 g (1¹/₄ oz)

Milk powder 10 g (¹/₃ oz)

Custard powder 10 g (¹/₃ oz)

Butter 60 g (2 oz)

Coconut cream 1 tsp

Full cream milk 1 tsp

Condensed milk 1 tsp

Vanilla essence 1–2 drops

1 Combine custard ingredients in a bowl. Mix well and steam over medium heat for 30 minutes, stirring occasionally during the cooking process.

2 When custard dries up into a thick paste, remove from heat and stir well again. Set aside to cool before dividing into 25 portions, rolling each one into a ball. Cover with cling film and chill in the refrigerator for 20–30 minutes.

3 Meanwhile, roll dough into a long cylinder. Divide dough into 25 equal pieces.

4 Lightly flatten each piece into a 0.5 cm (¹/₄ in) thick round disc. Scoop a ball of custard filling onto the centre of a dough round. Seal filling and roll into a ball. Repeat until all ingredients are used up.

5 Leave buns to prove for 45 minutes. Steam for 4 minutes over high heat.

6 Heat oil in a wok. Deep-fry custard buns until golden brown.

7 Serve immediately.

Egg Tarts Dan Ta

❀ Makes about 30 tarts

INNER CRUST

Salted butter 70 g (2¹/₂ oz)

Shortening 220 g (7⁴/₅ oz)

Hong Kong flour 200 g (7 oz)

OUTER CRUST

Hong Kong flour 120 g (4¹/₃ oz)

Bread flour 40 g (1¹/₃ oz)

Custard powder 10 g (¹/₃ oz)

Egg 1

Water 90 ml (3 fl oz / ³/₈ cup)

*SYRUP

Sugar 50 g (1²/₃ oz)

Water 75 ml (2¹/₃ fl oz)

CUSTARD

Eggs 90 g (3¹/₅ oz)

Syrup* 80 ml (2¹/₂ fl oz)

Evaporated milk 12 ml (²/₅ fl oz)

Vanilla essence 1–2 drops

Yellow colouring 1–2 drops

1 Prepare dough for inner crust. Mix all ingredients for inner crust until a smooth dough forms. Roll out dough into a 20 x 30-cm (8 x 12-in) sheet. Line the base of a baking tray with cling film. Lay dough flat onto the baking tray. Refrigerate for 20 minutes.

2 Prepare dough for outer crust. Add dry ingredients for outer crust into a mixing bowl and make a well in the centre. Add egg and water into the well. Mix until a smooth dough forms. Roll out dough into a 20 x 30-cm (8 x 12-in) sheet.

3 Press outer crust dough on top of chilled inner crust dough. Refrigerate for another 10 minutes.

4 On a floured surface or a clean dry towel, fold the crust into three parts. Flatten dough with a rolling pin. Repeat three times. Roll out dough until 0.5 cm (¹/₄ in) thick.

5 Cut out dough rounds with a round cutter of 5-cm (2-in) diameter. Press each dough round into a fluted tart tin. The dough should be about 0.5 cm (¹/₄ in) above the tart tin.

6 Preheat oven to 250°C (475°F).

7 Prepare syrup. Mix sugar and water and boil until it thickens. Leave to cool before mixing with the custard ingredients. Pour custard into the crusts until about 80 per cent full.

8 Bake egg tarts for about 15 minutes or until the crust turns crisp and brown. Serve immediately.

Found in Europe and Asia, this popular snack has also made its way to dim sum menus. It takes some effort to make the crust, but it will be worth it.

The crust for these delicious lotus rolls is the same as the egg tart pastry. Serve these warm to enjoy the combination of crispy crust and smooth lotus paste.

Lotus Rolls Lian Rong Su

🌸 Makes about 40 rolls

Pastry (see page 96)

Lotus paste 150 g (5$\frac{1}{3}$ oz)

Egg yolk 1, beaten

White sesame seeds for garnishing

Golden syrup or honey for glazing

1 Prepare pastry by following Steps 1–4 on page 96.

2 Preheat oven to 200°C (400°F).

3 Place lotus paste near the bottom edge of the pastry dough and roll it up into a long cylinder.

4 Starting at one end of the roll and slicing at a 45-degree angle, cut the roll into equal pieces.

5 Brush each roll with egg yolk before baking for 10 minutes, until the pastry turns golden brown.

6 Meanwhile, fry sesame seeds until fragrant.

7 Brush golden syrup or honey over baked lotus rolls and sprinkle over sesame seeds.

8 Serve immediately.

Leaf Cookies Ye Zi Bing

🌸 Makes about 25 cookies

Lotus paste 200 g (7 oz)

Egg yolk 1, beaten

Golden syrup or honey for glazing

PASTRY

Planta margarine 100 g (3½ oz)

Icing (confectioner's) sugar 35 g (1¼ oz)

Egg 1

Hong Kong flour 200 g (7 oz)

Colouring 1–2 drops, or as desired

1. Prepare pastry. Mix margarine and sugar until well incorporated. Mix in egg. Add flour, followed by colouring. Knead until a smooth dough forms. Leave dough to rest for 10 minutes.

2. Divide dough into 25 portions. On a floured surface, flatten each portion by hand until about 0.5 cm (¼ in) thick.

3. Preheat oven to 200°C (400°F).

4. Wrap lotus paste inside each dough portion and mould into a teardrop shape.

5. Lightly flatten each teardrop until it is in the shape of a leaf.

6. Impress lines to resemble veins on each leaf. Gently pinch the bottom while making a few light dents along the edges to resemble the jagged sides of a leaf.

7. Brush over with egg yolk before baking for 8 minutes, until cookies have browned.

8. Glaze cookies with golden syrup or honey and serve immediately.

These are lotus paste cookies that are great as snacks. The leaf shape adds an interesting touch, making this perfect for entertaining guests before or after a meal.

This recipe combines crunchy walnuts with buttery pastry to make fragrant walnut cookies that are also familiar to western cultures.

Walnut Cookies He Tao Su

🌸 Makes about 25 cookies

Lotus paste 300 g (10 1/2 oz)

Walnuts 50 g (1 2/3 oz)

Egg yolk 1, beaten

Golden syrup or honey for glazing

PASTRY

Hong Kong flour 300 g (10 1/2 oz)

Baking powder 2 g (1/15 oz)

Sugar 130 g (4 2/3 oz)

Custard powder 7 g (1/5 oz)

Milk powder 7 g (1/5 oz)

Eggs 2

Baking soda 2 g (1/15 oz)

Shortening 50 g (1 2/3 oz)

Butter 70 g (2 1/2 oz)

1 Prepare pastry. Sift flour with baking powder into a mixing bowl. Mix in the rest of the pastry ingredients. Stir to mix until a smooth dough forms. Set dough aside to rest for 20 minutes.

2 Divide dough into 25 portions. On a floured surface, flatten each portion by hand until about 0.5 cm (1/4 in) thick.

3 Preheat oven to 200°C (400°F).

4 Wrap lotus paste inside each dough portion and mould into a rectangular shape.

5 Press walnuts into the sides of each cookie.

6 Brush cookies with egg yolk before baking for 10 minutes, until cookies turn golden brown.

7 Glaze cookies with golden syrup or honey and serve immediately.

Butter Cookies Niu You Su

❀ Makes about 45 cookies

Red bean paste 300 g (10¹/₂ oz)

Egg yolk 1, beaten

Golden syrup or honey for glazing

PASTRY

Butter 200 g (7 oz)

Icing (confectioner's) sugar 70 g (2¹/₂ oz)

Eggs 2

Hong Kong flour 400 g (14 oz)

Desired colouring 1–2 drops,
    or as desired

1 Prepare pastry. Mix butter and sugar until well incorporated. Mix in eggs and flour. Stir to mix evenly until a smooth dough forms.

2 Add colouring and mix evenly. Leave dough to rest for 10 minutes.

3 Divide dough into 45 portions. On a floured surface, flatten each portion by hand until about 0.5 cm (¹/₄ in) thick.

4 Wrap red bean paste inside each dough portion and roll into a ball.

5 Preheat oven to 200°C (400°F).

6 Lightly flatten each ball and gently nip all around the middle with a pair of tweezers. Form another layer of ridges above the first layer by nipping in a circle. Continue to form layers of ridges all the way to the top.

7 Brush cookies with egg yolk before baking for 10 minutes, until cookies turn golden brown.

8 Glaze cookies with golden syrup or honey and serve immediately.

The classic butter cookie is enhanced by the addition of sweet red bean paste in this recipe.

GLOSSARY

Bean Curd Skins

Bean curd skins are a product of yellow soy beans and have high nutritional value. A popular ingredient in Chinese cuisine, bean curd food products are also hailed as "the meat in vegetarian food" because it contains proteins, dietary fibre and carbohydrates. Bean curd skins are used to wrap meat and other filling, which makes a very savoury and fragrant dish whether it is steamed or fried. Those available in the supermarkets are heavily salted. For the recipes in this book, it is best to use plain unsalted bean curd skins. To seal the filling more securely, use beaten egg or flour mixture to dab the edges before sealing.

Chinese Sausage

Chinese sausage is a common ingredient in Guangdong, Hong Kong, Macao and the southern regions of China. It is usually made of pork, which is minced and then packed into a lining made from pork intestines. The sausages are then compressed and dried, among other procedures, before they are ready for use.

Coriander

Coriander, or Chinese parsley, contains a beneficial volatile oil that gives it a pleasant aroma. It is this oil that counters the strong or gamey smell of meat, as well as the fishy taste in seafood. This herb lends a unique and fragrant flavour to dishes, and is a popular ingredient in dim sum either as part of a filling or as a garnishing.

Custard and Green Tea Paste

Custard (left) is a rich yellow paste used in sweet desserts like custard buns and pastries. When making your own custard, it is important to note that custard powder is a key ingredient. Custard powder gives a richer colour and flavour to the paste, and it cannot be substituted with other ingredients. Custard buns are a traditional favourite among the Cantonese, who like to enjoy this sweet treat during breakfast. Green tea paste (right) was traditionally not part of dim sum desserts. It was included much later on due to the increasing demand for green tea products, as research shows that green tea contains antioxidants that can slow aging and prevent cancer. The green tea paste used in dim sum is usually sweetened to suit the palate of dessert lovers.

Fermented Black Beans

These are essentially soy beans that are steamed and then left to ferment. It has a sharp salty taste and is a popular seasoning ingredient in Chinese cooking. Rinse with hot water before use to remove excess salt and dirt. Use sparingly and to taste, as they are high in salt content, and therefore very salty.

Ginger

Ginger is an important spice and herb to the Chinese. It has a strong spicy flavour that adds a pleasant taste to dishes. Ginger has a fresh fragrance that helps to remove the fishy taste of seafood and the pungent smell in meats. It does not overpower the main dish, rather, ginger enhances its flavour. Apart from its uses in cookery, ginger has long been regarded as a remedy for colds and motion sickness.

Glutinous Rice

Glutinous rice is sticky when cooked. The stickiness is a result of its high starch content. It is a variety of short-grained rice, and is commonly used in Chinese cuisine, especially for dim sum. Glutinous rice is said to contain more fat compared to its other rice cousins, and therefore considered a less healthy option. The dishes that use glutinous rice also contain salt, meat and oil, like the popular *lor mai kai* and glutinous rice in lotus leaf. Despite its less-than-healthy reputation, glutinous rice dishes remain a perennial favourite because of their savoury fragrance. However, as with most other types of food, glutinous rice, if consumed in moderation, will not cause major health problems.

Hong Kong Flour

Hong Kong flour is finer than other types of flours. It also contains less protein than plain (all-purpose) flour. It is a typically used for baked food like cakes and biscuits, and is particularly popular in Asian pastries because of its delicate texture.

Lotus Leaf

The lotus leaf comes from the aquatic lotus plant. The Chinese regard it as a herb with medicinal benefits that include antibacterial properties and the ability to dispel "heatiness" within the body. Lotus leaves impart fragrance to food, and is used in dim sum dishes like the *lor mai kai* and glutinous rice in lotus leaf.

Mushrooms

Mushrooms are versatile, and usually any type of Chinese mushrooms can be used in a dish, so you can pick the variety to use as desired. Chinese mushrooms are sold fresh or dried in most supermarkets. Dried mushrooms need to be reconstituted by soaking in water for about 20 minutes or until soft. Mushrooms are said to have health benefits like lowering cholesterol and preventing cancer.

Red Bean Paste and Lotus Paste

Red bean paste (left) is commonly used in East Asian desserts. It is dark red and has a sweet taste. The paste is made from skinned red beans, which are crushed and then boiled until they are mushy. The paste is then sweetened before it is cooked again to remove excess moisture. Like the red bean paste, lotus paste (right) is also common in Chinese cuisine as a dessert filling, in particular, Cantonese-style dim sum. To make lotus paste, lotus seeds are first boiled in water until they soften, then drained and mashed. Next, sugar and oil are added before cooking the paste in a pot or wok to remove excess moisture. Maltose is then added to make the final product.

Siew Mai Skins

These are essentially the same as wonton skins, and the thinner they are, the better. Their surface is also coated with a white powdery substance to prevent sticking. They are best stored sealed and chilled in the refrigerator to prevent them from drying out. Use the skins as soon as possible after opening, as they dry rather quickly. Store-bought skins are usually thick, so, just before using, it is best to apply pressure onto the stack of skins to flatten them, and then trim away the cracked edges.

Spring Onion (Scallion)

While it is a common and ordinary ingredient in Chinese cuisine, the spring onion has great nutritional benefits. It contains vitamins and minerals that are good for the body. It also imparts fragrance and enhances flavours of meats, especially when mixed together as a filling for dumplings, buns and other meat dishes. Spring onion can also be used as a garnishing. The amount to add for each dish varies, and can be adjusted according to personal preference.

Spring Roll Skins

Spring roll skins are not just used for wrapping the filling of spring rolls. They are crispy when deep-fried, making them good for other deep-fried snacks such as deep-fried wonton and pomegranate-shaped prawns. It is also used for popular snacks like samosa. The main ingredients for spring roll skins are high-gluten flour, water and eggs. They are sold in square sheets, and are available in most supermarkets.

Wafer Paper

These are thin sheets of wrappers made from rice, and are translucent and snowy white in colour. Good for making deep-fried snacks, wafer paper has a mild pleasant taste that does not overpower its filling.

Wheat Starch

This is a staple ingredient in dim sum, as it is used for dishes like *har kow* and blossom dumplings to form the translucent crystal-like skin. It also forms part of the batter in dishes like yam cake and carrot cake.

White Radish

A popular ingredient in Chinese cooking, the white radish is also key to the classic dim sum favourite, the carrot cake. It has vitamins, minerals and dietary fibre. There are different ways to cook the white radish. For example, it is also common to cook radish slices in soups and stews.

Yam

There are different varieties of yam, and the one pictured here is the preferred variety for dim sum snacks. The recipes in this book use the flesh of this type of yam, as it forms a smoother batter. Longer slimmer yams can also be used, but they tend to produce lumpy batter for dishes like yam dumplings and yam cake. Yam can be cooked in various ways, such as boiling, steaming, grilling, roasting, stir-frying or deep-frying. It is a good source of energy as it contains a significant amount of starch. Be careful when peeling yams, as they release a sticky substance that can irritate the skin, making it red and itchy. Wear gloves when handling yam and wash your hands thoroughly afterwards to prevent skin irritation.

Wonton Skins

Wonton skins can be square or round sheets of wrappers. They also come in two colours, yellow and white. Their surface is coated with white powdery flour, which prevents sticking. When sealing a wonton or dumpling, moisten the edges with water before pressing gently to secure.

WEIGHTS and MEASURES

Quantities for this book are given in Metric, Imperial and American (spoon) measures. Standard spoon and cup measurements used are: 1 tsp = 5 ml, 1 Tbsp = 15 ml, 1 cup = 250 ml. All measures are level unless otherwise stated.

LIQUID AND VOLUME MEASURES

Metric	Imperial	American
5 ml	$1/6$ fl oz	1 teaspoon
10 ml	$1/3$ fl oz	1 dessertspoon
15 ml	$1/2$ fl oz	1 tablespoon
60 ml	2 fl oz	$1/4$ cup (4 tablespoons)
85 ml	$2^1/2$ fl oz	$1/3$ cup
90 ml	3 fl oz	$3/8$ cup (6 tablespoons)
125 ml	4 fl oz	$1/2$ cup
180 ml	6 fl oz	$3/4$ cup
250 ml	8 fl oz	1 cup
300 ml	10 fl oz ($1/2$ pint)	$1^1/4$ cups
375 ml	12 fl oz	$1^1/2$ cups
435 ml	14 fl oz	$1^3/4$ cups
500 ml	16 fl oz	2 cups
625 ml	20 fl oz (1 pint)	$2^1/2$ cups
750 ml	24 fl oz ($1^1/5$ pints)	3 cups
1 litre	32 fl oz ($1^3/5$ pints)	4 cups
1.25 litres	40 fl oz (2 pints)	5 cups
1.5 litres	48 fl oz ($2^2/5$ pints)	6 cups
2.5 litres	80 fl oz (4 pints)	10 cups

DRY MEASURES

Metric	Imperial
30 grams	1 ounce
45 grams	$1^1/2$ ounces
55 grams	2 ounces
70 grams	$2^1/2$ ounces
85 grams	3 ounces
100 grams	$3^1/2$ ounces
110 grams	4 ounces
125 grams	$4^1/2$ ounces
140 grams	5 ounces
280 grams	10 ounces
450 grams	16 ounces (1 pound)
500 grams	1 pound, $1^1/2$ ounces
700 grams	$1^1/2$ pounds
800 grams	$1^3/4$ pounds
1 kilogram	2 pounds, 3 ounces
1.5 kilograms	3 pounds, $4^1/2$ ounces
2 kilograms	4 pounds, 6 ounces

OVEN TEMPERATURE

	°C	°F	Gas Regulo
Very slow	120	250	1
Slow	150	300	2
Moderately slow	160	325	3
Moderate	180	350	4
Moderately hot	190/200	370/400	5/6
Hot	210/220	410/440	6/7
Very hot	230	450	8
Super hot	250/290	475/550	9/10

LENGTH

Metric	Imperial
0.5 cm	$1/4$ inch
1 cm	$1/2$ inch
1.5 cm	$3/4$ inch
2.5 cm	1 inch

All photos by Liu Hongde, Hongde Photography

First published in 2014 as *Cooking Classics: Dim Sum*
and *Dim Sum Basics* in 2019
This new edition 2022

Published By Marshall Cavendish Cuisine
An imprint of Marshall Cavendish International

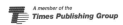

A member of the
Times Publishing Group

Limits of Liability/Disclaimer of Warranty: The Author and Publisher of
this book have used their best efforts in preparing this book. The parties
make no representation or warranties with respect to the contents of this
book and are not responsible for the outcome of any recipe in this book.
While the parties have reviewed each recipe carefully, the reader may not
always achieve the results desired due to variations in ingredients, cooking
temperatures and individual cooking abilities. The parties shall in no event
be liable for any loss of profit or any other commercial damage, including but
not limited to special, incidental, consequential, or other damages.

Other Marshall Cavendish Offices:
Marshall Cavendish Corporation, 800 Westchester Ave, Suite N-641,
Rye Brook, NY 10573, USA • Marshall Cavendish International (Thailand)
Co Ltd, 253 Asoke, 16th Floor, Sukhumvit 21 Road, Klongtoey Nua,
Wattana, Bangkok 10110, Thailand • Marshall Cavendish (Malaysia) Sdn
Bhd, Times Subang, Lot 46, Subang Hi-Tech Industrial Park, Batu Tiga,
40000 Shah Alam, Selangor Darul Ehsan, Malaysia

Marshall Cavendish is a registered trademark of Times Publishing Limited

National Library Board, Singapore Cataloguing-in-Publication Data

Name(s): Ng, Lip Kah.
Title: Dim sum basics : irresistible bite-sized snacks made easy / Ng Lip Kah.
Description: New edition. | Singapore : Marshall Cavendish Cuisine, 2022.
| First published in 2014 as: Cooking classics: dim sum and Dim sum basics
in 2019.
Identifier(s): ISBN 978-981-5044-11-9 (paperback)
Subject(s): LCSH: Dim sum. | Cooking, Chinese.
Classification: DDC 641.5951--dc23

Printed in Singapore